CELTIC TRAVELLERS

SCOTLAND IN THE AGE OF THE SAINTS

DONALD SMITH

THE STATIONERY OFFICE

Published by The Stationery Office and available from:

The Stationery Office Bookshops
71 Lothian Road, Edinburgh EH3 9AZ
(counter service only)
South Gyle Crescent, Edinburgh EH12 9EB
(mail, fax and telephone orders only)
0131-479 3141 Fax 0131-479 3142
49 High Holborn, London WC1V 6HB
(counter service and fax orders only)
Fax 0171-831 1326
68-69 Bull Street, Birmingham B4 6AD
0121-236 9696 Fax 0121-236 9699
33 Wine Street, Bristol BS1 2BQ
0117-926 4306 Fax 0117-929 4515
9-21 Princess Street, Manchester M60 8AS
0161-834 7201 Fax 0161-833 0634
16 Arthur Street, Belfast BT1 4GD
01232 238451 Fax 01232 235401
The Stationery Office Oriel Bookshop
The Friary, Cardiff CF1 4AA
01222 395548 Fax 01222 384347

The Stationery Office publications are also available from:

The Publications Centre
(mail, telephone and fax orders only)
PO Box 276, London SW8 5DT
General enquiries 0171-873 0011
Telephone orders 0171-873 9090
Fax orders 0171-873 8200

Accredited Agents
(see Yellow Pages)

and through good booksellers

The Stationery Office
South Gyle Crescent
Edinburgh EH12 9EB

Applications for reproduction should be made to
The Stationery Office

Photographs on page numbers 8, 9, 11, 15, 19, 23, 24, 25, 27, 29, 31, 32, 35, 39, 40, 41, Crown Copyright: reproduced by permission of Historic Scotland.
Photographs on page numbers 4, 13, 34, : © RCAHMS
Photographs on page numbers 18, 43: © The Trustees of the National Museums of Scotland, 1997
Cover photograph by Stephen Kearney and Paul Watt
The Eildon Hills from Scott's View.

Acknowledgements
The publisher acknowledges with thanks; Historic Scotland, Royal Commission on the Ancient and Historical Monuments of Scotland, Royal Museums of Scotland, Stephen Kearney and Paul Watt for access to and use of photographs throughout this book

All facts have been checked as far as possible but the author and publishers cannot be held responsible for any errors, however caused

British Library Cataloguing in Publication Data

A catalogue record for this book is available from the British Library

Printed in Scotland by CC no 70343, 80c 2/97
Designed by Jim Cairns Design

ISBN 0 11 495829 7

CONTENTS

The Ruthwell Cross, detail

CELTIC TRAVELLERS

WHEN WAS SCOTLAND?

The political unit which we now call Scotland did not emerge until the ninth century. Before that there were four main racial and cultural groupings each of which maintained their independence. These were the British of Strathclyde and Galloway, the Picts who occupied the largest part of Scotland, the Scots of Dalriada who raided and then settled in Argyll from Ireland, and the Anglo-Saxons of Northumbria who pushed into southern Scotland. From about 800 AD a fifth group, the Norse of Norway and Denmark, harried and then colonised large areas of northern Scotland and the Western Isles.

Of these now five groups, three - the Picts, the Scots and the British - were Celtic peoples, though belonging to different branches of the Celtic language tree. The Norse and Germanic peoples were also racial cousins but nonetheless bitter enemies in the struggle for land and power. In areas settled by the Anglians and the Norse a sub-stratum of the Celtic peoples continued to exist and in due course to mix with the invaders.

The Viking invasions of the ninth century were a major catalyst towards the formation of a single Scottish kingdom. First the Picts and Scots united under one royal dynasty (though not without continuing coups and feuds) and then the British Kingdom of Strathclyde was annexed and its royal elite driven into exile in Wales. By this time the spread of Christianity was a significant common factor in the cultural make-up of the diverse yet related peoples of northern Britain.

WHO WERE THE SAINTS?

The Early Saints were Scotland's first missionaries and the direct successors of the missionaries or apostles who were instructed by Jesus, the founder of the Christian faith, to live a life of travel, poverty, teaching and healing in the service of God.

More specifically the early Saints flourished between the foundation of Whithorn around 400AD and the sack of Iona by the Norse Vikings around 800AD. The successors of the early Saints were the Culdees or 'companions of God', the monks and clerics who maintained the Celtic traditions of the missionary churches until the reigns of Queen Margaret and her pious sons. While respecting the spirituality of the native Church, Margaret paved the way for the introduction of continental models of parish and monastic life. An interesting variation on this pattern is Norse Christianity which did not develop in Scotland until the ninth century.

Most people know the names of St Columba of Iona and St Ninian of Whithorn but may be less familiar with St Cuthbert, St Brigid, St Moluag, St Ethernan, St Hilda, St Drostan, St Maelrubha, St Fergus and a host of others. This is a pity because the later prestige of two or three 'big names' has obscured the multi-coloured mosaic which makes up Scotland's spiritual geography. Every area has its particular names and associations and this mosaic reflects not just the origins of Christianity but early patterns of settlement, travel, place names and cultural roots. The early Saints are a pathway to understanding our mixed British, Irish, Pictish, Anglo-Saxon and Norse inheritance.

WHAT WAS CELTIC?

Celtic is not an exact description of the Early Saints but it is a useful shorthand for what was distinctive about apostolic Christianity in Scotland, Ireland and Wales.

Travel had a particular significance for the Early Saints since they obeyed literally the command to take the Christian Gospel 'to the ends of the earth'. They were motivated by a spiritual hunger to reach a new frontier by sea or land and to discover a 'place of resurrection' where their own vocation would be fulfilled. This impulse took these intrepid travellers to the west of Ireland, the Western Isles of Scotland, Orkney, Shetland, the Faroes and Iceland. Their sea-haunted settlements can still be traced today.

Behind this adventure of exploration was a penitential spirit which began in the monasteries of Egypt. Irish texts speak of the three orders of martyrdom - the white martyrdom of exile, the green martyrdom of solitude, and the red martyrdom of blood sacrifice. No-one viewing the rocky hermitages on North Rona and the Farne Islands, or the monastery at Kame of Isbister on Unst can doubt the authenticity of the self-sacrifice involved. Nor, given the turbulent tribal culture of war and raiding, can we doubt the courage of these advocates of a new faith and a new social understanding.

At the same time the Early Saints did not deny the beauty and goodness of life. For them the natural world breathed the Spirit of God the Creator. Their perception was intense, as if concentrated by spiritual discipline, and the veil between the seen and unseen worlds was rubbed thin, and suffused with light. But the Early Saints were also successful missionaries, and the introduction of Christianity was not achieved without practical sense in addition to spiritual vision. In many ways these first missionaries defined themselves in relation to the existing primal and tribal religions, adopting their best practice while clearly foregrounding the moral and spiritual superiority of the new faith. Standing stones became cross-slabs and high crosses, while cells and chapels were established in places which were already religious centres. Existing power structures were also utilised and the patronage of chiefs and kings sought for Christianity. The Early Saints strove to place a new value on every human life and gradually promoted an ethic of kindness amongst warrior aristocracies.

Finally the Early Saints expressed their faith through the culture of the people amongst whom they worked. Partly this was an instinctual preference since the Saints were by and large themselves Celts, but it was also a conscious strategy to ensure that Christianity took root. The Celtic respect for learning and tradition was continued, though the oral traditions were now supplemented by the writing skills of the monks. The Celtic sense of form and colour found new inspiration and patronage in carved crosses, illuminated manuscripts and intricate metalwork. Poetry and music, which were the time-honoured ways of praising earthly rulers, were now employed to praise the High King of Heaven.

This book has been produced in 1997 to mark the 1600th anniversary of the first mission to Whithorn, later associated with Ninian, and the 1400th anniversary of Columba of Iona. That however is only a threshold to some of the journeys briefly outlined in these pages. A good road atlas is essential and ordnance survey maps will assist detailed exploration. A pilgrimage is a journey which involves some kind of discovery, in the travelling or the arriving. This text is a point of departure.

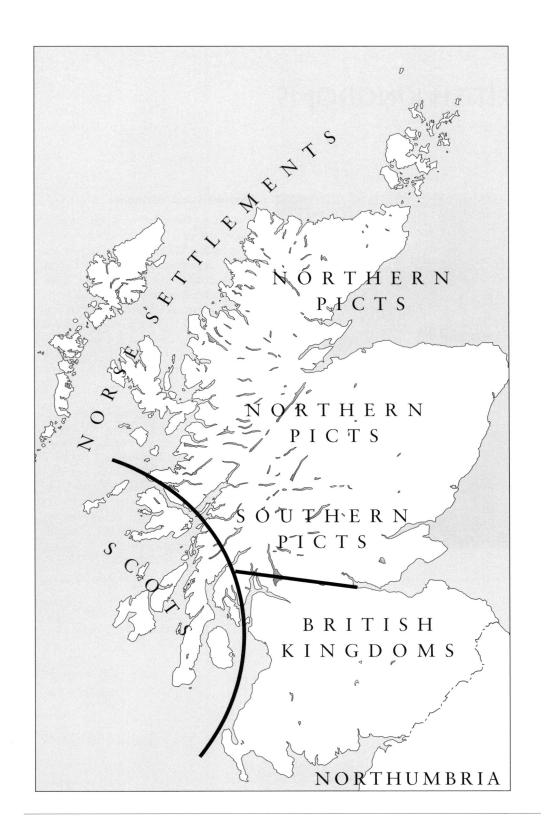

THE BRITISH KINGDOMS

The Ruthwell Cross

Ruthwell and Hoddom

To the west and north of Annan, these two places formed a meeting point between three ancient kingdoms and two peoples - the Britons of Galloway and Strathclyde, and the Anglians of Northumbria. Now preserved in Ruthwell Church with an accompanying exhibition, a magnificent seventeen foot high carved stone cross was originally sited on the shore, and may have marked a literal and symbolic frontier. It is one of the finest early Christian monuments in Europe.

By contrast Hoddom conceals its significance beneath a later castle and church, and a strangely shaped hill crowned by a watchtower. This however was the pivot of Saint Kentigern's mission north into Strathclyde and south into the Lake District. When Kentigern met King Rhydderch of Strathclyde here the ground rose up in the shape of the hill to provide the crowds with a view.

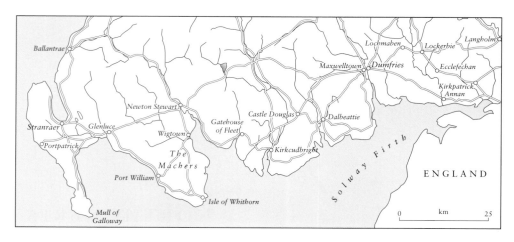

Whithorn

Founded in the early fifth century by Ninian, Whithorn is the first cradle of Scottish Christianity. The later priory church and the museum and discovery centre look down on the site of the recent excavations, which revealed a bustling early monastic and missionary centre. Ninian's 'Candida Casa' or 'Shining House' was named from the white plastered walls of his church which copied the early Gallic churches. The church was dedicated to Martin of Tours by whom Ninian is believed to have been influenced. Whithorn was a centre of royal pilgrimage until the time of the Reformation.

St Ninian's Cave

Like many Celtic Saints, Ninian had a refuge or 'dysart' (desert place) from his busy cares as a Bishop, missionary and teacher. Carved cross slabs from the cave are in the priory museum but early crosses are still visible on the cave walls, now partially collapsed. The cave is revived as a place of modern pilgrimage.

Isle of Whithorn

Overlooking the harbour, St Ninian's Chapel served pilgrims arriving by sea. The view from this rocky promontory takes in the Lake District and the Isle of Man - a good reminder of Whithorn's strategic position on the western seaways. Traces of an earlier Celtic enclosure are visible around the medieval ruins. Further up the coast, five miles north-west of Port William, is another pilgrims chapel, Chapel Finian, serving pilgrims arriving from Ireland.

Pilgrim Routes: the Coast Road

Those not arriving by sea might follow the coast road from Ayr and Prestwick, cutting across by Loch Doon or the valley of the River Cree. Robert the Bruce came this way seeking a cure for his leprosy. Overcome by weariness he thrust his spear into the

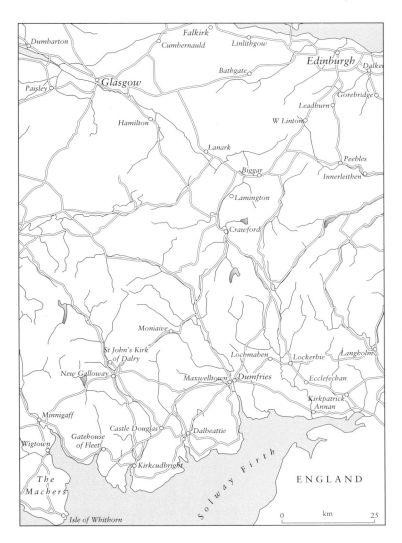

ground and a well sprang up. So he founded a leper hospital and a Chapel of St Ninian, whose ruins can still be seen in Prestwick beside Bruce's Well.

Pilgrim Routes: Overland

An even more popular route was followed by the Stewart Kings of Scotland in their regular pilgrimages from the capital at Edinburgh. James I to V all came this way as did Mary Queen of Scots. The road ran from Wigtown to Minigaff, New Galloway, St John's Kirk of Dalry, Moniaive and Kirkton at Crawford, and then on to St

St Ninian's Chapel

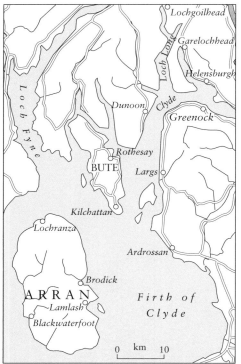

Ninian's Kirk and St Ninian's Well at Lamington, Biggar Collegiate Church and so to Edinburgh. James IV was famous for bringing a retinue of minstrels and other entertainers, turning his pilgrimage into a festive progress. The route north via Crawford was also Kentigern's in his day, turning west towards the Clyde Valley and Glasgow. The shady burial ground by the river at Kirkton, just north of Crawford, was dedicated to the British Saint Constantine and still breathes something of its early atmosphere.

Kirkmadrine and Kirkmaiden

Whithorn's fame has partially obscured the equal claims of the Rhinns of Galloway to be the home of Scotland's earliest Christian settlement. At Kirkmadrine the outstanding collection of early Christian sculptures includes two fifth century gravestones with probably the earliest Christian crosses to have been carved in Scotland after the departure of the Roman legions. Nothing remains of the monastery which once stood here.

Further down the Rhinns, towards the Mull of Galloway, is Kirkmaiden, the Chapel or Church of Medana, which looks over the waters of Luce Bay. On the shore, below the surviving medieval church, is a well also dedicated to Saint Medana who plucked out her own eyes rather than succumb to the attentions of an Irish Prince who was a slave to their beauty. The eyes were thrown out to sea where they became the Scares rocks halfway across to Whithorn.

Kilwinning

Kilwinning is the church of Wynnin (in its British form) or Finan (in its Irish form). It is a marker of the way in which the early missionaries moved westwards into the British Kingdom of Strathclyde from the Firth of Clyde. Kilmarnock and Kilmaurs to the west; Kilbirnie, Lochwinnoch, Kilbarchan and Kilmacolm to the north-west; and West Kilbride on the coast, all indicate early Celtic church settlements. The abbey at Kilwinning, like Kilbirnie Old Kirk, is a later building on or near the original foundation.

Ardrossan to Arran

The ferry from Ardrossan arrives at Brodick, the best place to begin exploration of Arran's ancient landscape and many prehistoric remains. On the west side of the island is the Kilbrannan Sound named after St Brendan the Voyager. A ferry crosses from Lochranza to Claonaig in Kintyre. Arran has its own Saint, Molaise, nephew of Saint Blane. Two miles north-east of Blackwaterfoot is Shiskine Church, the burial place of Molaise. The remains of the Saint's shrine can still be seen in the church. Molaise's retreat or 'dysart' was on Holy Island off Lamlash. His cave is on the west side of the island which also has a number of early rock carvings. Boat trips are available from Lamlash and Whiting Bay. Holy Island is a contemporary place of religious retreat cared for by Buddhist monks.

Largs to the Cumbraes

The coastal resort of Largs has associations with Columba, who is traditionally supposed to have made a landfall in Largs Bay below the present St Columba's Church. Largs is also a ferry point for Great Cumbrae Island. Both of the Cumbraes were an integral part of the network of Celtic settlements and sea routes embracing Arran, Bute and Kintyre. The Episcopal Cathedral of Argyll and the

Isles in Millport contains some early Celtic crosses, and claims to be Britain's smallest cathedral. St Beya, also known as St Vey, had her retreat on Little Cumbrae.

Wemyss Bay to Bute

The island of Bute was a major centre for the early Saints and is dotted with ruined chapels and Celtic dedications. Some have argued that it is the 'Island of Delights' visited by the ancient Irish St Marnoc in 'The Voyage of Brendan'. On the west side, the remote chapel of Kilmichael and Michael's grave overlook the Kyles of Bute in peaceful beauty. The connection here may be with an almost forgotten St Michul rather than with Michael. To the south-east lies Kilbride Hill and the chapel or kil of Bride. Further south on St Ninian's Point, St Ninian's Chapel looks across to Inchmarnock which also has a ruined church dedicated to St Marnoc.

Even more important is the south end of the island where Kilchattan Bay commemorates a contemporary of Columba, St Catan, whose nephew Blane is now Bute's most famous saint. The remains of St Blane's chapel and monastery are remarkable and include the cashel or enclosing wall, the foundations of an early Celtic chapel, a well, traces of the first monks' huts or cells, an extensive cemetery which may include Blane's grave, and a strange early fort or broch now called the Devil's Cauldron, as well as the medieval church. Set among cliffs and trees, the monastery looks out to sea.

Paisley and Renfrew

The magnificent cathedral and modern industrial town of Paisley grew originally around an early Celtic settlement. Paisley's saint is another missionary, St Mirren, whose chapel can be found in the cathedral. Note also the stone carved Barochan Cross. Renfrew is associated with St Convall whose grave is believed to be at the modern church of Inchinnan, on the west side of the town. Both Saints are part of the westward movement of the Irish Scots from Dalriada.

Glasgow

Despite strong Irish and Highland influences on the city, Glasgow in early times was a British Celtic settlement. St Ninian may have established the first Christian cemetery here while Kentigern (better known by his nickname Mungo) came cross-country from Culross to Glasgow along the Campsie Fells. The ancient church site at Govan is also dedicated to a British saint, Constantine. The medieval Cathedral of St Mungo is still one of Glasgow's splendours, now complemented by the adjacent St Mungo Museum of Religious Life. The site of Mungo's shrine is in the crypt below the High Altar. The People's Palace on Glasgow Green has an excellent display on the early history of Glasgow, including its Celtic origins. A magnificent stone carved sarcophagus in Govan Old Parish Church may have formed part of St Constantine's shrine.

Dumbarton

Dumbarton Rock was the capital of the Kingdom of Strathclyde - the 'dun' or fortress of the Britons. Now surmounted by much later fortifications, it still guards the northern approaches by land and sea. Recent scholars favour a Lake District rather than a Strathclyde origin for St Patrick the apostle to the Irish, but dedications to British saints such as Old Kilpatrick and Kilmahew Chapel at Cardross (Mayhew was a companion of Patrick) indicate the character of the area in the age of the Saints.

Luss

On the west side of Loch Lomond the lovely village and church of Luss are associated with an early missionary from Ireland, St

St Blane's Chapel

Dumbarton Rock

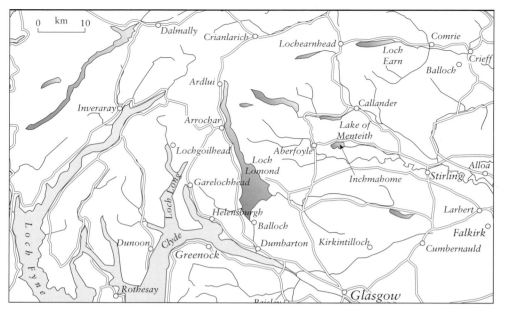

Kessog. Kessog was a popular local saint whose activities stretched from the Cumbraes to Callander, and whose relics were revered well beyond the Reformation. A medieval carving of Kessog can be seen at Luss while an icon of Kessog was recently installed in St Kessog's Church in Balloch. Tradition has it that Kessog was martyred overseas but his body was brought back to Loch Lomondside wrapped in sweet smelling herbs. Luss is Gaelic for 'herb'. Kessog's retreat was probably on Monks' Island in the Loch.

Balmaha

At the south-east corner of Loch Lomond the national nature reserve opens out from Balmaha. From this frontier area of British Strathclyde the intrepid early missionaries moved into the Trossachs and the territories of the Southern Picts. The largest island in Loch Lomond, Inchmurrin, is named after Saint Mirren who had a retreat here, while Inchcailloch off Balmaha is associated with St Kentigerna. An Irish royal princess, Kentigerna worked with her brother St Comgan around Loch Alsh, but then withdrew to become a recluse on Inchcailloch, which means 'island of the old

women'. The chapel on this island, which can be reached by boat from Balmaha, became the burial place of the MacGregors.

The Campsies Route

If Kentigern first came to Glasgow along the foot of the Campsie Fells, then this was also a route by which the Scottish Saints of Dalriada travelled east. The route followed was close to that of the Romans' Antonine Wall, running from Old Kilpatrick through Bearsden, Kirkintilloch, Kilsyth and Falkirk to Bo'ness on the Forth estuary. Falkirk owes its development to Saint Medan or Modan. Blanefield may mark the north-eastern progress of Blane's missionary journeys from Bute. There is a St Mirren's Well at Kilsyth.

Inchmahome

From Port of Menteith a boat plies across to Inchmahome, the largest island on the Lake of Menteith. The present ruins date from the 13th to 16th centuries but this green and peaceful retreat recalls the first Christian settlement on this island of Colmaig or Colman, a little-known Scottish missionary venturing east and north into the territory of the Southern Picts.

THE SCOTS OF DALRIADA

The Kildalton Cross

Keil and Sanda

The Mull of Kintyre is a stepping stone between island and mainland Scotland. One tradition is that Columba's first Scottish landfall was at Keil Point, where a later church and a St Columba's well are still to be seen. The rock cut footprints (only one of which is genuinely old) have some unknown ritual significance. Caves to the west mark an early settlement.

Sanda, which can be reached by boat from Southend, is associated with Ninian and a ruined chapel can be seen on the island. Sanda is approximately midway between the Ailsa Craig and Ayrshire to the east, and Rathlin Island and Ireland to the west.

Campbeltown and Kintyre

Before its absorption into the empire of Clan Campbell, the main town of Kintyre was Kinlochkerran - the head of the loch of St Ciaran, an early missionary from Ireland. On one of his journeys Columba encountered a trading ship here from Gaul - modern-day France.

The Campbeltown Museum outlines the notable part played by Kintyre in the settlement of the Scots from Ireland and the emergence of the kingdom of Dalriada, though many of the peninsula's visible church remains date from the later Lordship of the Isles. Saddell Abbey on the east coast has a notable collection of medieval Celtic sculpture, while at Skipness the ruined church of St Brendan looks down the Kilbrannan Sound to Arran. At Tayinloan on the west a car ferry crosses to Gigha

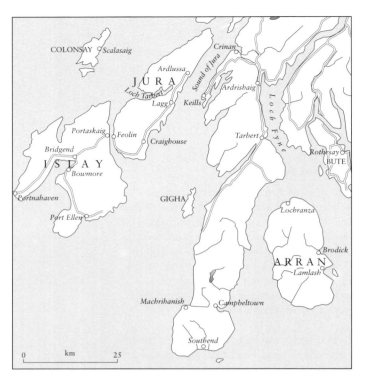

Tarbert to Islay (Port Askaig)

West of Port Askaig is Loch Finlaggan and the island named Eilean Mor ('Big Island'). This was at one time the capital of the Lordship of the Isles, but originally the retreat of St Findluggan who threw himself between Columba and a spear but escaped unscathed. The view east to the Paps of Jura has the austere grandeur of the Hebridean 'dysart'.

The Rhinns of Islay are especially rich in traces of the Early Saints due to their strategic position on the sea route between Ireland and Scotland north of the Great Glen. Kilchoman at Rockside and Kilchiaran are the two most important sites. Kilchoman has a fine carved cross while the sheltered bay at Kilchiaran provided safe haven for the Saints' currachs. By contrast, Kilchoman looks starkly out over empty miles of ocean.

Islay to Jura

A car ferry runs from Port Askaig to Feolin on Jura. The 'big sea bag' of Loch Tarbert in Jura fits Adomnan's description in his 'Life of Columba' of the island of 'Hinba'. The caves on the north shore of the loch may have housed the penitential retreat on Hinba. Killernadale to the south of Loch Tarbert is dedicated to Columba's uncle, St Ernan, who was a Prior of Hinba and wished, according to tradition, to be buried on Jura.

At Tarbert itself the ruined church and graveyard of Kilmahoire contain an earlier chapel of Columba and there is a Columba's Well to the east of the cemetery. Was this where Columba, as described by Adomnan, received his most sacred visions over a period of three days and nights?

Loch Caolisport

In Knapdale north of mainland Tarbert, the road to Ellary passes two caves, which became early centres of Christian worship.

(Norse: 'God's Island'), whose oldest church site at Kilchattan is dedicated to St Blane's uncle, St Catan.

Tarbert to Islay (Port Ellen)

A 'tarbert' is a crossing place or narrow isthmus where boats could be dragged overland. A car ferry to Islay runs from Kennacraig to Port Ellen or Port Askaig.

Seven miles east of Port Ellen is the Kildalton Cross, the only High Cross to survive complete in its original site and the most intensely Celtic of all these magnificent crosses. The monastery at Kildalton was dedicated to 'the Fosterling', who may have been Columba's foster son and successor St Baithene. Columba's last words as he died transcribing Psalm 34 were 'Let Baithene finish it'. Between Kildalton and Port Ellen is the little island of Texa which was an early monastic site and visited by St Cainnech or Kenneth who is also remembered at Inchkenneth off Mull.

A stone altar, carved crosses and a font indicate 'St Columba's Cave'. A later medieval chapel is sited by the shore.

Kilmory Knap and Eilean Mor

A footpath from Ellary is the most direct route to the chapel at Kilmory and its medieval stone carvings including the MacMillan Cross. The chapel is dedicated to St Maelrubha of Applecross, missionary to the north-west.

From Kilmory you look down to St Cormac's Chapel on the island Eilean Mor. Cormac was a voyaging saint who travelled north to Orkney and beyond.

Dunadd and Kilmartin

Dunadd was the principal fortress of the Kingdom of Dalriada. Columba may have installed Aidan as King on the rock where a carved footprint and stone basin have some ritual significance.

To the east of Dunadd is the church of Kilmichael Glassary where in 1814 workmen discovered a bronze bell shrine containing a seventh century Celtic handbell. It is now in the National Museum in Edinburgh and may be the bell of St Moluag, which was long treasured on Lismore.

Between Dunadd and Kilmartin, three miles to the north, lies one of the richest concentrations of prehistoric sites in Scotland. Kilmartin Church has a fine collection of early carved stones, while Kilmartin House is an attractive visitor centre with a display on Celtic sea travel.

Cowal

The hil-girt narrow-shored peninsula of Cowal, intersected by sea lochs, is remarkable for the number of early Christian sites still occupied by present day churches. These include Strachur, Kilfinan, The Church of the Three Holy Brethren at Lochgoilhead, and Kilmodan. There are also a large number of abandoned turf-covered enclosures and foundations indicating other places of early missionary settlement. On either side of the river at Strathlachlan are Kilmure and Kilbride. Harder to find but nonetheless rewarding is Fearnoch near Colintraive - a very early chapel ruin set in a hidden dell 500 metres north-west of the main road surrounded by hills which were then covered with oak trees. By contrast St Conan, the Saint of Cowal, is commemorated on a grand scale by the modern St Conan's Church on the shores of Loch Awe, near Dalmally.

The MacMillan Cross

The Garvellachs and Scarba

These uninhabited islands are still among Scotland's most inaccessible places, yet in the context of the Early Saints they are as spiritually important as Iona. Travel is via Seil and car ferry to Luing from where summer boat trips are available.

Scarba is a steep-sided island with dangerous whirlpools to north and south. At the north-east landing place of Kilmory are the remains of the monks' beehive cells like those at Skellig Michael off Ireland. These are places of penance and spiritual challenge.

The Garvellachs are if anything rougher and rockier than Scarba. Eilean An Naoimhe ('the Saint's Isle') has often been claimed as Columba's holy island of Hinba, but before Columba, St Brendan the Voyager established the precarious monastery of Ailech here. The site with its beehive cells, chapel and underground store certainly belongs to the Brendan tradition of seagirt isolation. The next island is Cuil Breanainn or 'Brendan's retreat' and it in turn is close to the largest island, whose main hill is called Dun Breannain -'the hill of Brendan'. And everywhere the sound of the sea.

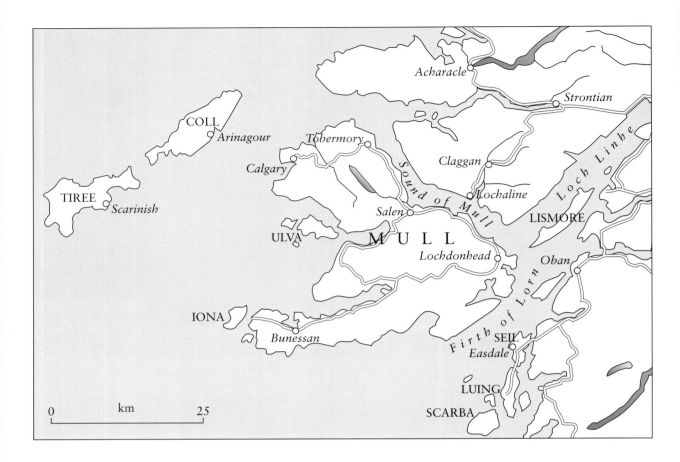

Oban to Iona

Mull is one of the largest and most beautiful of Scotland's islands with its fair share of early chapels and settlements such as those at Pennygown near Salen, Dervaig and on Inchkenneth. Nonetheless the focus is on Iona, the site of Columba's principal monastery and the burial place of Scottish Kings for many centuries. Travel is by car ferry to Craignure, road to Fionnphort and ferry to Iona. The pure gentle light of Colum Cille's Isle contrasts strongly with the rugged salt-scoured Garvellachs.

On Iona, St Oran's Chapel and burial ground may commemorate an earlier foundation than that of Columba. Columba's monastery was to the north of the present restored Benedictine Abbey, but only its cashel or enclosing wall survives. Tor Abb, a mound to the west of the Abbey, is believed to be the site of Columba's own cell, while the gravestone known as 'Columba's Pillow' is housed in St Columba's Shrine in the Abbey or cathedral church.

The restored Abbey buildings are the base of the twentieth century Iona Community, founded by George MacLeod to take the gospel of Columba into urban Scotland. The High Crosses of St Martin and St John, though partially restored, are among Scotland's finest Celtic artworks.

Every feature on Iona has an association with Columba. Adomnan's *'Life'* is essential reading for its radiant portrait of life in the days of Columba and his successors. From here the Saint's spiritual influence reached out through Dalriada and eastwards to the Kingdoms of the Picts. To the north-west the flat fertile acres of Tiree and Coll were ideally suited to serve Iona as a granary, and several working communities were established on these islands.

Oban to Colonsay and Oronsay

On Oronsay, which is reached from the larger island of Colonsay by a tidal causeway, are the impressive ruins of a fourteenth century priory dedicated to Columba. The tradition is that Columba landed here in 563 but pressed on to Iona because he could still see Ireland from the summit of Beinn Oronsay. At Kilmory, 80 metres south of the track to the Priory, are the remains of a very early chapel.

Similar remains are evident at several sites on Colonsay including Upper Kilchattan and St Catherine's Chapel beyond Balnahard at the north end of the island. Colonsay House is built on the site and probably with the stones of Kiloran, the main church settlement on Colonsay. It was dedicated to St Oran, so underlining the links with Iona.

Lismore

In the mouth of Loch Linnhe, the island of Lismore (ferry from Port Appin) is a strategic link between Oban, Appin, Morvern and Ardnamurchan beyond. It was also a pivot between the Kingdom of Dalriada and Pictish territories to the north. The island was an important burial place and is stippled with cairns.

Legend has it that Columba and St Moluag raced for possession of Lismore but that Moluag cut off his little finger and threw it ahead to ensure his claim. It is interesting that Columba and Moluag both arrived shortly after the defeat of the Scots of Dalriada by Brude, the overlord of the Northern Picts. Of the two saints Moluag

has the greater claim as an apostle to the Picts with early dedications reaching from Lewis in the west to Rosemarkie and Aberdeen in the east.

Lismore's visible remains hardly reflect its early importance. There is a ruined chapel associated with Columba on Bernera at the south-west end of Lismore. Portmoluag is where Lismore's patron Saint first landed, and his principal monastery and burial ground were at Clachan around the surviving church. It and the visible foundations around it, however, belong to the later Cathedral of the Isles which stood within the 'great enclosure' or 'lios mor' of Moluag's monastery from which the island takes its present name. Moluag's own staff survives and is kept on Lismore by its Hereditary Keeper.

In the sixteenth century Scotland's greatest collection of Gaelic poetry, '*The Book of the Dean of Lismore*', was compiled in this centre of Gaelic culture. The Saint himself was celebrated in poetry as 'Moluag the clear and brilliant, the sun of Lismore in Alba'.

Loch Etive and Loch Leven

To the south and north of Lismore the sea lochs of Loch Etive and Loch Leven offer access to the east. Ardchattan Priory on the north shore of Loch Etive is a medieval foundation on an earlier Celtic site, dedicated to St Catan of Bute.

East of Ballachulish in Loch Leven is Eilean Munde, the island of St Munnu or Fintan Munnu, a cousin of Columba who is believed to have been a leper. The chapel on this lovely island is a burial place of the MacDonalds. Munnu is also remembered around Loch Fyne and his staff was preserved at Kilmun on the Holy Loch. Irish tradition remembers Munnu as 'a warrior, religious, and tortured with pain'.

SOUTH-EASTERN FRONTIERS

St Fillan's Crosier, in the Royal Museum of Scotland

Lindisfarne

Lindisfarne, later known as Holy Island, is a tidal island north of Bamburgh, ancient capital of the Anglian kingdom of Northumbria. The first monastery on Lindisfarne was founded from Iona at the invitation of King Oswald, who had spent several years there in exile. The ruined Priory and the present church are both much later in date but still exude the spirit of place characteristic of Celtic sites. The church at Bamburgh is dedicated to St Aidan, who led the successful mission from Iona.

The most famous Prior of Lindisfarne was St Cuthbert, who also had a chapel on the tidal Hobthrush Rock south-west of the village. Cuthbert's body was reverenced here until the Viking onslaught forced the monks to take their Saint's relics on a tortuous pilgrimage, ending up finally at Durham where Cuthbert's shrine can be visited today.

Lindisfarne began a creative fusion of Celtic and Anglo-Saxon culture which bore fruit in the Lindisfarne Gospels, the Ruthwell Cross, the poetry of Caedmon, and Bede's Life of Cuthbert. A visitor centre at the Priory places Lindisfarne in its historic and cultural context.

The Farne Islands

Cuthbert was a reluctant leader of the Northumbrian Church. Before becoming a monk at Old Melrose he may have been a shepherd in the Scottish Borders. Something of that spiritual independence brought him in his Christian vocation to the Farnes.

Above, St Ninian's Cave

Below left, carved footprint at Dunadd

Below right, St Mungo's Cathedral, Glasgow

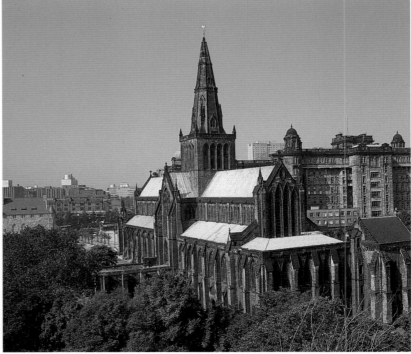

Access to these rocky outposts, which vary from 15 to 28 in number depending on the tide, is by boat from Seahouses. The islands are bustling with bird life and a resort for seals, and tradition abounds with stories of Cuthbert's close friendship with his fellow creatures, especially his favourite eider ducks which are still called 'Cuddy's Chickens'.

Bede describes Cuthbert's little cashel or enclosure with his cell, a guest house and a little garden sheltered from the worst of the sea spray. The medieval St Cuthbert's Chapel stands on the site of the guest house, but not even Celtic hospitality could have softened the austerity of this retreat.

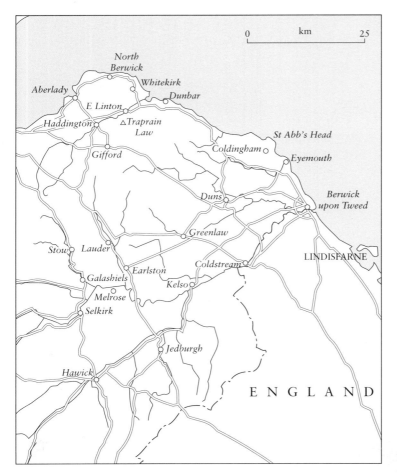

Coldingham and St Abbs Head

The sheer headland of St Abbs takes its name from the Anglo-Saxon princess Ebba, who founded a monastery here at the top of the 300-foot cliffs. Only a few windswept traces remain between St Abbs Head and Coldingham Loch. An old Northumbrian rhyme goes,

St Abbs upon the Nabbs
St Helens upon the Lea
St Bees upon Dunbar Sands
Stands closest to the Sea.

This refers to the supposed shipwreck of three Anglo-Saxon princesses off Dunbar, after which each one founded a monastery— at St Abbs, on the shore near Cockburnspath where a St Helen's Church still stands, and at Dunbar. In fact St Bee or Bega was an Irish missionary who worked closely with St Hilda of Whitby and St Ebba. The medieval church at Dunbar was dedicated to Bega.

Despite her Anglo-Saxon origins, Ebba's monastery was a thoroughly Celtic foundation combining men and women, which may be the reason for later criticism of her 'laxness'. Cuthbert used to stay here ,slipping down to the shore to spend the night hours in penitential prayer waist-deep in water. One night a young monk watched Cuthbert emerge in the dawn hours numb with cold, but two otters came out of the sea to rub his frozen limbs with their waterproof fur.

After the Viking onset, St Abbs was destroyed, but St Margaret's son King Edgar re-established the monastery inland at Coldingham where extensive remains including the lovely parish church of Coldingham Priory can still be visited.

Traprain Law

The hump-backed hill of Traprain was an Iron Age fortress guarding the coastal route north. A British tribe, the Votadini, had their stronghold here in Roman times and a hoard of silver was buried on the Law during the unsettled period of the Roman withdrawal.

Legend has it that Loth, the British King who gave Lothian its name, cast his pregnant daughter Thanew (also known as Enoch) down the hill in a chariot but the axle jammed and somehow she survived. Thanew was a Christian who had refused marriage to a British prince by whom she had then been raped. Next Thanew was cast off in a boat at Aberlady but she sailed safely over to the Isle of May (followed by all of Aberlady's fish!) and then to Culross where her baby was brought up by St Serf to become St Kentigern. Behind this legend lies the beginnings of Christian faith amongst the British tribes of southern Scotland. The geography of the tale is clearly visible from Traprain on a good day.

Whitekirk and North Berwick

North of Traprain Law is the medieval pilgrimage centre of Whitekirk. The sacred well here was deliberately blocked up but a modern annual pilgrimage from Whitekirk to the 'Lamp of Lothian', St Mary's Church at Haddington, proves that ancient traditions have a surprising power of renewal.

The coast between Dunbar and North Berwick was the haunt of the east coast hermit Saint Baldred. St Baldred's Cradle, a rock off the coast at Tyninghame, was according to story originally between the Bass Rock and the shore but in response to Baldred's prayers God shifted it south. Below Tantallon Castle, St Baldred's Boat is another coastal landmark while the Bass Rock itself was the Saint's retreat. Successively a religious 'dysart', fortress, prison and nature reserve, the rock can be viewed by boat trip from North Berwick. Continuing towards Edinburgh, Aberlady was an early Christian settlement with Northumbrian connections.

Edinburgh

Scotland's present capital began life as a Bronze Age and then Iron Age fortress on Castlehill with a complementary settlement on Arthur's Seat. From here warriors of the British and Christian kingdom of Gododdin marched south to be wiped out at Catterick by the Anglo-Saxons - an event still remembered in Scotland's oldest surviving poem *The Gododdin*. Subsequently King Edwin of Northumbria established his northern frontier here.

Beneath rich layers of later history, Edinburgh's early religious sites include St Cuthbert's Church and graveyard at the west end of Princes Street Gardens and St Triduana or St Modwenna's Well at Restalrig. Triduana is supposed to have skewered her own eyes on two thorns rather than be forced to marry a Pictish king, and her well was supposed to cure blindness. In Edinburgh Castle, St Margaret's Chapel commemorates the founding mother of Scotland's medieval Church. Though she looked to European Catholicism for her organisational model Margaret was a devout admirer of Celtic spirituality, which is reflected in the chapel's modern windows, and in its pure simplicity.

The Royal Museum of Scotland includes in its collection many Celtic treasures including the Monymusk Reliquary of St Columba, and St Fillan's Crozier.

South Queensferry to Inchcolm

Further along the Forth Estuary, past the superb Norman church of Dalmeny, is Queensferry from where pilgrims passed over the river to St Andrews courtesy of St Margaret. The pilgrims' ferry left from the Binks near the medieval church of St Mary of Mount Carmel. The modern pier at the other end of South Queensferry is the departure point for the *Maid of the Forth* which sails to North Queensferry and Inchcolm.

Inchcolm Abbey is the most complete monastic ruin in Scotland and includes the original cell (though much restored) of the hermit monks, beginning with Colm who may have given the island its name. Stranded on Inchcolm, Alexander I (another son of St Margaret) was so impressed by the then hermit's humble hospitality that he vowed to found a monastery here. Since he was known for his devotion to St Columba, King Alexander may have begun the identification of Colm with Columba which led to the island being known as the Iona of the East.

Abercorn

Often forgotten is the secluded yet accessible church of Abercorn which was a Celtic monastic settlement and for a brief time the centre of a Northumbrian bishopric. Apart from a beautiful Anglo-Saxon cross-shaft, the visible remains are all of a later date but the peaceful atmosphere evokes a spiritual antiquity. The Northumbrians had to abandon the site when a major defeat at the hands of the Picts swept their northern frontier southwards.

The Upper Tweed

If the coast road from Lindisfarne to Edinburgh was the conduit of Anglo-Saxon influence, the mainland routes south across the hills were the continuing spheres of British and later Scottish culture. In the time of the Early Saints the overland routes were guarded by a series of hill forts.

Going south by Penicuik, where the church is dedicated to Kentigern or Mungo, you reach the Tweed at Peebles. This area has associations with four early missionaries: Bega, Kentigern, Llolan and Ronan. East of Peebles down the Tweed at Innerleithen is St Ronan's Well. Little is known about the historical Ronan who is nonetheless celebrated through Sir Walter Scott's novel 'St Ronan's Well'.

Turning West at Peebles, you can follow the Tweed to the old kirk at Stobo and then on to Drumelzier, where Kentigern is supposed to have met and baptised Merlin shortly before the great magician's death. North of Drumelzier at Broughton, the old church contains in its grounds a very early saint's cell associated with Llolan, a little-known British Saint. Llolan's bell and staff were once kept by the Earls of Perth at Kincardine-on-Forth, and the Celtic handbell in the Glasgow Museums collection may be Llolan's.

The approach to Broughton from the Tweed Valley is guarded by the prominent hill fort at Dreva from where you can follow the Broughton Burn north or easily cross westwards to Biggar and another major north-south route. Remaining in the Tweed Valley south of Drumelzier, the early missionary sites have the same frontier quality. The remote hillside church and well at Kilbucho were dedicated to St Bega, an Irish missionary whose travels down the Tweed valley are remembered in several place names. At the upper reaches of the Tweed east meets west.

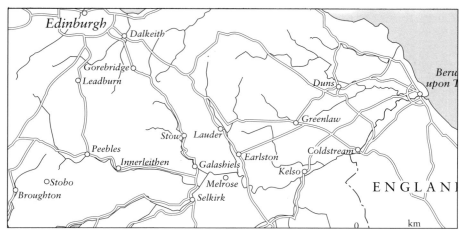

Above, St Margaret's Chapel, Edinburgh Castle

Right, Inchcolm Abbey

Below, St Andrew's Cathedral with St Rule's Tower from the harbour

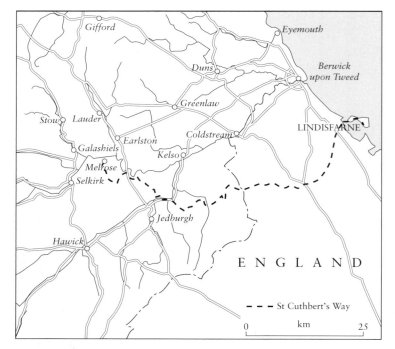

St Cuthbert's Way

From Melrose a recently established walkers' route can be followed for 62½ miles all the way to Lindisfarne. The route is fully waymarked with the symbol of St Cuthbert's Cross, but the Trail Guide is essential since some of the paths and tracks are not on older maps.

The route links full circle Cuthbert's British origins in the Borders with his later life and work in the Anglo-Saxon Kingdom of Northumbria, while taking in many places of historic interest and rugged natural beauty. St Cuthbert's Way also connects the northern endpoints of the Southern Upland and Pennine Ways.

Jedburgh

Leaving Edinburgh by a third overland route (the modern A68) you pass over Soutra Hill. At the summit, commanding an extensive view across the Forth Estuary, was an important medieval hospital. The route continues through Lauder, across the Tweed between Melrose and Dryburgh to Jedburgh Abbey, 6 miles north of the present border between England and Scotland.

The Abbey is built on the site of an early Christian settlement which was originally a missionary outpost of Lindisfarne. In a major excavation in 1984 archaeologists discovered many early carved stones, Anglo-Saxon coins, and part of an elaborately carved shrine for the body of a Saint. Many of these finds are on display in the Abbey's first-rate visitor centre.

The ruins of Jedburgh Abbey tower dramatically above the road north, but its border position was to cause its monastic community much suffering during the wars between England and Scotland. The Saints of Southern Scotland and Northumbria were making peace along this route centuries before Scotland or England existed as separate kingdoms.

Dryburgh Abbey

The Tweed Valley

Going south from Edinburgh by Dalkeith and Borthwick, the road follows a medieval pilgrims' route to Melrose via Stow and the Gala Water. The monastery of Mailros or Old Melrose was on a bend of the Tweed 2½ miles east of the Abbey ruins. It was probably founded by St Aidan of Lindisfarne with monks from Iona, and its first Abbot was Eata, one of Aidan's Anglo-Saxon converts.

Nearby St Boswells is named after the first Prior of Old Melrose, St Boisil. He was also the first to recognise Cuthbert's spiritual gifts when the young countryman came to join the monastery.

Further down the Tweed is Dryburgh Abbey, tucked inside a bend of the river and screened with trees. The medieval abbey was built on the site of St Modan's cell or chapel in the very first phase of missionary endeavour among the Britons. Amidst the ruins is a vaulted Chapel of St Modan, which was originally the monks' library and vestry.

KINGDOMS OF THE SOUTHERN PICTS

Dunfermline and Culross

At Dunfermline St Margaret, a Saxon princess, married the Scottish King Malcolm. The nave of Dunfermline Abbey stands above Margaret's Church of the Holy Trinity which in turn replaced a Celtic church. St Margaret's Cave, now off the Glen Bridge Car Park, was the Queen's retreat.

West of Dunfermline, Culross was the centre of St Serf's missionary endeavours among the Southern Picts. His monastery was probably on the site of the present Abbey at the top of the town. On the shore east of Culross, the ruins of the medieval St Mungo's Chapel are a reminder that St Kentigern was born here and brought up by Serf.

The Ochils

Serf's missionary journeys can be followed by connecting up the early church sites which bore his name. At Clackmannan the parish church stands on the site of an earlier St Serf's church, while the clach or stone which is displayed in the square, and from which the town takes its name, may be a survival from pre-Christian worship of the sea god Mannan or Manau.

At Hawkhill, in the grounds of Alloa Park south of the Clackmannan road, there is a Pictish burial marked by a sandstone block with a sculptured cross. To the northwest was the major hill fortress of the Maetae (now Dumyat) which stood guard over this early Pictish kingdom.

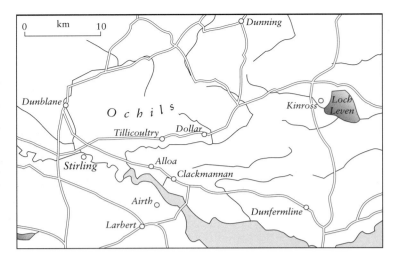

and overlooks Strathearn which has different missionary connections.

Alternatively, continuing east at the Yetts o'Muckhart you reach Loch Leven where on St Serf's Island the ruins of a later priory, which was built on the site of a Celtic monastery, can be visited from Kinross.

Dunblane

North of Stirling, but south-west of Serf's church at Dunning, is the modestly magnificent Cathedral of Dunblane. The original Celtic monastery was founded here by St Blane, possibly on the hillside above the present cathedral. Poised over the River Allan, Dunblane commands the missionary routes north and south. The visitor centre in Cathedral Square, Archbishop Leighton's Library, and the reconstructed chapel behind Scottish Churches House all add to Dunblane's standing as a historic and contemporary place of faith.

The Fife Coast

From North Queensferry the road passes above Dalgety Bay and the narrow passage to Inchcolm Island with its medieval Abbey. At Aberdour the beautiful parish church is dedicated to St Fillan but is Norman in origin. In Burntisland the original parish dedication was to St Serf, but the handsome parish kirk is an early post-Reformation building. At Dysart, now annexed to Kirkcaldy, the ruined medieval church of St Serf stands near the harbour. Dysart was the 'desert' or retreat of St Serf and his cave is a stone's throw from the church in the grounds of Dysart House, which is now a Convent. Here, according to tradition, St Serf was assaulted by the Devil.

Beyond Dysart are the Wemyss Caves, which contain the largest accumulation of prehistoric and Early Christian rock carvings in Britain. Unfortunately the combined effects of erosion, coal mining and vandalism have blocked access to many

Continuing on Serf's route, the Medieval church at Tullibody was dedicated to St Serf and St Kentigern. Further up river the 'field of Kenneth' at Cambuskenneth (possibly the site of a battle) later became the location of the medieval Abbey of Cambuskenneth. On the other side of the Forth, the old kirk at St Ninian's may be a genuine foundation of Ninian of Whithorn, marking the northward progress of his mission to the Picts.

Serf's own influence kept to the north side of the Forth, emanating from the important early site of Logie at Airthrey, which nestles below Dumyat adjacent to the modern University of Stirling. The oldest visible building here is medieval but the life of Saint Serf records a visit here and the old church and graveyard bear all the hallmarks of an early Celtic site.

From Airthrey the road follows the foot of the Ochils where medieval churches at Alva and Tillicoultry were dedicated to Serf. Beyond Dollar at the Yetts o' Muckhart a steep road goes up Glen Devon and over the Ochils to Dunning, where the early medieval St Serf's Church survives complete with its tower. St Serf is reputed to have slain a dragon at Dunning in the spot still called the Dragon's Den. Dunning seems to mark the westerly limits of Serf's influence,

*Right, Inchmahome
Priory, Lake of Menteith*

*The Barochan Cross,
Paisley Abbey*

*Left, Suenno's Stone,
Forres*

*Below, Dunblane
Cathedral*

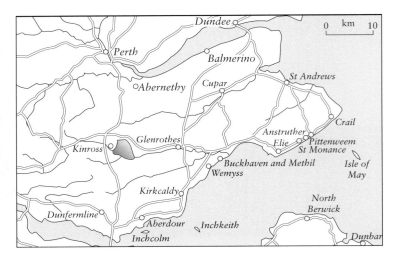

by the Vikings but his church became the centre of a healing cult which was given royal status after David I was cured here of a troublesome arrow wound.

Pittenweem means 'the town of the cave' and is named after the famous cave by the harbour which is associated with St Fillan. The Saint is supposed to have worked in the cave guided by a miraculous light from his left arm - the same arm which later became a sacred relic and was carried into battle at Bannockburn.

Here legend has superseded history, but the history is equally interesting. Excavations on the Isle of May, which is reached by boat from Pittenweem or Cellardyke, have discovered an early church and shrine beneath the later Priory buildings. This may be the burial place of St Ethernan, an early Irish missionary who founded several churches on the east coast of Scotland. St Ethernan also had a retreat in the caves at Caiplie between Cellardyke and Crail, but it was on the May that he and his community were killed by the Vikings. The Priory on the May became an important place of pilgrimage, later moving to Pittenweem where it is connected to St Fillan's Cave by a stairway cut in the rock.

Beyond the bustling fishing centre of Anstruther, Crail's fine medieval church is refuge to some early carved stones including an ornate Celtic cross slab. Beyond Crail is the easternmost point of the Neuk, Fife Ness. On the Ness a defensive fortification known as Dane's Dyke can still be seen and in the cave below, King Constantine is believed to have been put to death by his Viking conquerors.

St Andrews

The street plan of St Andrews is still that of a medieval pilgrimage centre, culminating in the ambitious Cathedral of St Andrew. But several layers of religious development lie behind that achievement.

of the carvings and obscured others. Care should be taken, and for an informed visit contact with the Wemyss Environmental Centre in East Wemyss is recommended.

The East Neuk

Largo Law stands guard over the access to the East Neuk of Fife, and a Pictish symbol stone can be seen at the church in Upper Largo. Coming down on the east side of the Law the road passes by Kilconquhar to Elie. Originally Elie was a landing place serving the church of Conchobar, or Kilconquhar, an important early monastery. Conchobar was an Irish missionary with relatively few Scottish associations.

St Monan, who gave his name to St Monans, was possibly a follower of St Ethernan, also known as Adrian, who left his community on the Isle of May to establish a lonely retreat in a small cave at Inverey, two miles west of Pittenweem. Alternatively, Irish monks may have brought the relics of a St Moineann here and created a shrine. St Monan's Cave, sadly filled in with concrete by the local council, was on the opposite side of the burn from the impressive medieval church of St Monan, which was built on the site of a much older church. St Monan was probably martyred

The early Celtic foundation was by St Kenneth, a friend of Columba, and marked a centre of mission to the southern Picts called Kilrymont. The cult of St Andrew was a conscious creation of the early Kings of the Scots and Picts, possibly based on some holy relics brought to Scotland by St Regulus or St Rule to whom an earlier church on the Cathedral site is dedicated. Alternatively, Regulus was another Scottish holy man already associated with this site, which seems to have grown in stages from a cave by the shore (St Rule's or Lady Buchan's Cave), to a church on Kirkhill, to St Rule's Church and the Cathedral.

The magnificent carved sarcophagus unearthed at the cathedral was certainly an object of early veneration, as well as one of Scotland's finest Celtic artworks.

Abernethy

The coastal route from St Andrews to Abernethy takes in the tranquil medieval Christian sites of Balmerino and Lindores Abbeys. Abernethy itself, however, was an ancient Pictish capital and the 74-foot high round tower indicates the importance which the Kings of the Scots and Picts placed on Abernethy as a religious centre. There is a persistent tradition that St Brigid or St Bride herself established a monastery here before Columba's mission to Scotland.

Stratherarn

From Abernethy it is a short distance to Bridge of Earn and then upriver to Forteviot where Constantine, one of the first monarchs to rule both the Picts and the Scots, established his capital at a prestigious Pictish centre. This might seem incredible today, were it not for the survival here of the elaborately carved Dupplin Cross which is certainly a regal monument. At the time of writing the cross is still in its original site behind Bankhead Farm on the B9112, but there are plans to move it to Forteviot Church for protection.

The River Earn continues towards Crieff while a network of minor roads traverse the Strath. Dunning is due south while at Muthil there is another early medieval church tower very similar to that of Dunning. At Aberuthven the old parish church was dedicated to St Catan.

North west of Madderty Church, which was dedicated to St Ethernan are the ruins of Inchaffray Abbey, which was established on another early Celtic site. St Fillan's armbone was kept here. On the northern edge of Strathearn is St Bean's Church at Fowlis Wester. St Bean was an Irish missionary who established his church at an existing religious centre, as the nearby Bronze Age cairn and standing stones vouchsafe. There are Pictish stones here as well, including the cross in the village square. The church itself is medieval.

From the bustling town of Crieff, Strathearn narrows towards the loch at its head. Crieff's mercat cross in East High Street marks this as another place of early missionary settlement. Loch Earn itself is associated with an earlier St Fillan than the Saint whose relics were so celebrated. At St Fillans, south of the river and beyond the golf course, is a ruined chapel and burial ground which is believed to be the site of St Fillan's cell. The rock of Dundurn three fields further on was occupied by a Pictish fort and later became known as St Fillan's Seat. At the other end of the Loch, near Edinample on the south side is a ruined chapel of St Blane.

Abernethy Round Tower

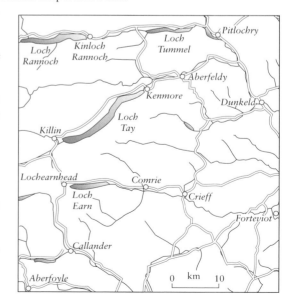

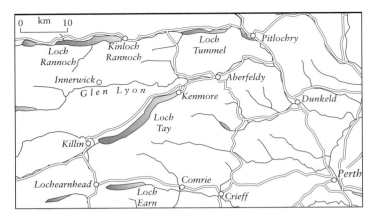

now houses the Breadalbane Folklore Centre. The Centre, like the mill before it, guards St Fillan's Healing Stones, each of which was applied to different parts of the body. The parish church at Killin is also on an early site and displays an ancient seven-sided font.

Glen Lyon to Aberfeldy

The best way into Glen Lyon is the Steep and narrow Ben Lawers road from Loch Tay, four miles out of Killin, to Bridge of Balgie. Adomnan established his settlement near here, west of the Pictish brochs at Cashlie, in Milton Eonan – the mill town of Adomnan.

At Innerwick the little church houses an early saint's handbell which is ascribed to the Anglo-Saxon missionary St Cedd. Intriguingly, the old church at Foss near Tummel Bridge, one glen north of Glen Lyon, was dedicated to Cedd's brother St Chad. Both brothers were trained by St Aidan at Lindisfarne.

Continuing down Glen Lyon you reach the hill at Camusvrachan where Adomnan drove out a plague from the local people into a rock. The rock and a cross slab still survive. Adomnan died in Glen Lyon, and his last wish was that his body should be carried along the river until the first thong or 'dul' broke. Hence he was buried at Dull in the mouth of the glen.

At Fortingall on the road to Dull there are standing stones, and in the churchyard a yew tree which is claimed to be three thousand years old. Legend has it that Pontius Pilate was born here and that a Pictish chief went to Rome with Pilate's father and heard St Peter preach. Certainly a Pictish Christian centre of learning was established at Dull on a site behind the church and attracted not only Adomnan but Cuthbert, and perhaps Cedd and Chad as well. Dull survived as a place of learning into Catholic times.

Glen Dochart

The story goes that St Fillan and St Adomnan came east together via Loch Etive and Glen Lochy to Tyndrum. There at the headwaters of the Tay they cast lots and Glen Lyon fell to Adomnan, Glen Dochart to Fillan. Adomnan's natural route would be over the old drovers road between Ben Dorain and Ben Odhar to Loch Lyon, and the site of an old chapel is still marked above this walker's route. From Tyndrum, Fillan would go south-east along the strath which bears his name.

Fillan's original monastery was either near St Fillan's Pool on the farm of Auchtertyre (the Pool is on the West Highland Way) or a mile further east where the ruins of the later St Fillan's Priory can be visited on Kirkton farm. The two sites are intimately connected through the healing cult of Fillan, since after being dipped in the pool mad people were bound, wrapped in straw and their heads laid in the stone font in the ruins with Fillan's bell placed above them. There they spent the night! St Fillan is traditionally believed to be buried here and his relics were reverenced in this area under the guardianship of their Dewars or hereditary keepers until the nineteenth century. St Fillan's Crozier and Bell are now in the Royal Museum of Scotland in Edinburgh.

At Killin on the western end of Loch Tay, Fillan established a mill whose successor

Ardchattan Priory

St Ninian's Chapel, Isle of Whithorn

St Serf's Church, Dunning

The Kildalton Cross, Islay

The Dunfallandy Stone

At Weem, two carved crosses from Dull are preserved in the old church, which was dedicated to St Cuthbert. He had a retreat in the cliffs above the village when he was at Dull.

From Aberfeldy it is possible to double back to Kenmore and Loch Tay. The loch has sites of early Celtic settlement on both shores as well as a series of crannogs or artificial islands. The largest of these is the Isle of Loch Tay, formerly Eilean nam Ban or the Island of the Women near Kenmore. Alexander I's Queen was buried on this ancient site and the ruins of a priory are still visible. Aberfeldy's own early dedications are to St Palladius or St Paldy, an Irish monk involved in the southern Pictish mission. St Paldy's Fair was held in the town.

Dunfallandy

From Logierait east of Aberfeldy a minor road goes north along the River Tummel to Dunfallandy. Near the old burial ground on the left hand side of the road, the Dunfallandy Cross is richly decorated with beasts and angels on one side, and Pictish symbols on the other.

Dunkeld

South from Aberfeldy and Pitlochry, Dunkeld was established as a religious site of national importance by Kenneth MacAlpin, King of the Picts and Scots. An earlier monastery here was linked with Iona and grew in importance because of Viking attacks on the mother house. Columba's relics were then divided between Dunkeld and Kells in Ireland. The present Cathedral and its satellite town are peacefully gathered between the river and the wooded mountains. An exhibition in the Chapter House sets the historical scene.

Scone

Just north of Perth is Scone Palace. An early religious settlement here was given major status by Kenneth MacAlpin who brought the sacred Stone of Scone to this site. The Kings of Dalriada had been crowned on the stone at Dunadd and then Dunstaffnage, and its placing here emphasised the importance of the new royal dynasty of the Scots and the Picts. Nothing is left of this period at Scone except the Moot Hill. After a seven hundred year forced sojourn under the throne in Westminster Abbey, the Stone of Scone has recently been returned to Edinburgh Castle, but will still travel south for coronations.

Meigle

North of the Sidlaw Hills at Meigle there is clear evidence of the rich Christian culture achieved by the Southern Picts before the advent of Kenneth MacAlpin's dynasty. The excellent museum at Meigle houses over thirty Early Christian carved stones which were discovered in or about the old churchyard. The stones marked places of worship, boundaries and perhaps spheres of clan and family influence. Their pre-Christian symbols are still not fully understood due to the lack of contemporary written evidence.

Glamis and Kirriemuir

The church at Glamis is on an early site associated with the Pictish missionary St Fergus. In the Den of Glamis near the church, St Fergus' Well has recently been uncovered and a beautiful woodland 'cathedral' created. A fine carved stone with an intricately interlaced cross stands in the manse garden. St Fergus may be the Pictish bishop who attended a Church Council in Rome in 721. His missions crossed Aberdeenshire into Caithness, where he is the patron Saint of Wick. His arm was reverenced in a shrine in St Machar's Cathedral in Aberdeen and his head in another shrine at Scone, but his burial place was at Glamis.

The old parish church in Kirriemuir is also an early Celtic site. Many of the carved stones found here are housed in the Forfar

Museum. Enthusiasts for Pictish carving might also seek out St Orland's Stone on Cossan's Farm - a hike east of the Glamis to Kirriemuir road - and the more accessible Eassie Stone in Eassie churchyard, two miles west of Glamis, which has another finely interlaced cross. An OS map is required for these expeditions.

Restenneth and Forfar

East of Forfar the fine ruins and imposing tower of the early medieval priory at Restenneth are associated with St Boniface, a Pictish Bishop also known by his Celtic name Curitan. It has been argued that Restenneth was originally founded by the Pictish King Nechtan who asked Abbot Ceolfrith of Jarrow to send him masons to build a stone church dedicated to St Peter, so reflecting the religious independence of the Pictish dynasties from Iona and Dalriada. Three miles south-east of Forfar is Dunnichen Hill where at the battle of Nechtansmere in AD 685 an even earlier Pictish monarch, King Brude, defeated the Angles of Northumbria and assured Scotland's freedom from Anglo-Saxon domination. In Forfar itself the Meffan Gallery accommodates the Art Gallery and Museum. The Forfar Museum has a fine collection of carved stones, many of which come from Kirriemuir and Menmuir.

Aberlemno and Brechin

Between Restenneth and Brechin, Aberlemno village and kirkyard have four early carved stones including two outstanding crosses. The stones are covered during the winter for protection. The Round Tower at Brechin Cathedral was originally an independent building used as a belfry, warning tower and refuge. The tower with its beautifully carved doorway and crucifixion reflects Irish ecclesiastical influence on the dynasty of Kenneth MacAlpin rather than the earlier Pictish Church. The cathedral itself is medieval, but its collection of carved stones recalls its original identity as a Celtic monastery.

The Mounth

North of Brechin the fertile lowlands known as the Mearns narrow towards the Mounth's strategic passage into Aberdeenshire. The medieval dedications to St Palladius, who is supposed to have ordained Serf at Auchenblae, and to Aberdeenshire's St Ternan at Arbuthnott point simultaneously south and north. The Pictish fortress at Bowduns, adjacent to Dunnottar Castle, guarded the approaches. The early dedication at Dunnottar to St Ninian pays tribute to his southern Pictish mission rather than to a personal foundation.

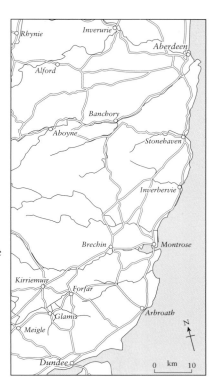

St Vigean's and Arbroath

Turning south on the coast road, via Inverbervie and Montrose, one of Angus' finest collections of Pictish Stones is reached at St Vigean's Museum in the suburbs of Arbroath. Dedicated to the Irish missionary St Fechan, this was clearly the site of a major Celtic monastery though the existing church is medieval. There are over thirty carved stones in the museum, including the famous Drosten stone with its still undeciphered inscription which may contain the names of both St Drostan and St Fergus. The prestige of this site was sustained in the splendour of Arbroath's medieval Abbe,y now sadly ruined.

Travelling south-west to Dundee, a detour to the Panmure Monument at Craigton takes in the free-standing Camus's Cross or Camustane which echoes the style of the Irish High Crosses. Due south of Craigton there was a Celtic monastery at Monifieth on the site of the old parish church, where Pictish slabs and a later cross-shaft were found in the nineteenth century.

KINGDOMS OF THE NORTHERN PICTS

The Nigg Cross

Fragment

Banchory

The obvious source of missionary influence on northern Pictland was the earlier established churches of the Southern Picts. St Ternan was a Pict who was baptised by St Palladius, the Irish missionary who also ordained St Serf. Ternan's main centre was at Banchory, where the medieval church of St Ternan occupies the likely site of his early monastery, opposite the existing church of Banchory, Ternan just above the river. This is not to be confused with Banchory, Devenick on the lower Dee, which was founded by St Devenic. A little-known colleague of St Machar, Devenic is believed to be buried at the site of the present church.

Milton of Tullich

North of Ballater is the scattered hamlet of Milton of Tullich where, below the main road, is the ruined medieval church of St Nathalan. There is also a collection of Pictish carved stones and an old font. Nathalan is remembered as an agricultural Saint who lost his faith when the crops failed. So he locked his working arm to his side and went on pilgrimage to Rome, having thrown the key into the Dee. But in Rome he bought a fish from a boy and in its stomach was the key. Nathalan also founded churches at Old Meldrum (Bethelnie) and Coull. He is supposed to be buried at Tullich.

The Upper Dee

The natural route into the upper Dee is by Glenshee and Glen Clunie. It seems likely that St Monire came this way, only to meet stiff opposition from the local population. Driven out of Auchendryne (on the site of modern Braemar) he retreated up the valley and crossing the Ey he sought shelter on Carn na Moine. There, after a night in the open, he was comforted by a pure spring welling up from the hillside.

Later Monire moved down the valley to Crathie, and the site of his chapel is still marked by a standing stone a mile beyond Abergeldie Castle on the south bank of the Dee. Polmanaire, a deep pool near Balmoral, is the pool of Monire and his well, now called Tobar Mhoire, still flows on the mountainside at Carn na Moine.

Old Aberdeen

Aberdeen's connection with the Early Saints is through the Cathedral of St Machar in Old Aberdeen. Machar was an Irish missionary who accompanied Columba to Dalriada and then moved east, establishing a chapel on the site of the later cathedral at a bend in the River Don.

From Aberdeen, a journey up the Don Valley confirms another missionary route. At Dyce, the ruined medieval church outside the village was dedicated to St Fergus and contains an early Pictish stone combining native symbolism and a decorated cross. At the church in Kintore there is another Pictish Christian stone as well as a pre-Reformation Sacrament House.

Branching away from the Don, Inverurie churchyard has a collection of early carved stones, while off the main road, one mile north-west of Chapel of Garioch, is the Maiden Stone with a fine Celtic Cross on one side and a rich sample of Pictish symbols on the other.

At Insch the old parish church was dedicated to St Drostan, while even further up-country at Rhynie the old graveyard south of the village has two fine Pictish symbol stones. On the summit of Tap 'o Noth, north of Rhynie, is the Stone of St Moluag - Clochmaloo - marking the route over the hills to Moluag's church at Mortlach near Dufftown.

Old Deer

The Celtic monastery at Old Deer was the strategic centre of the early Christian mission to Buchan. The monastery was probably on the site of the parish church in Deer rather than where the later ruins of Deer Abbey stand north-west of the village. The Book of Deer, preserved in Cambridge University Library, is a precious Celtic manuscript, written in Latin but annotated two centuries later in Scottish Gaelic.

The monastery was founded by St Drostan whose churches are spread over Aberdeenshire, Buchan and across the Firth in Caithness. An old Irish text speaks of 'Drostan and this three' which refers to St Fergus, St Medan and St Colm or Colman, all of whom are associated with early church sites in Buchan and Caithness. Few visible remains survive of this missionary movement. Drostan's main port seems to

The Maiden Stone

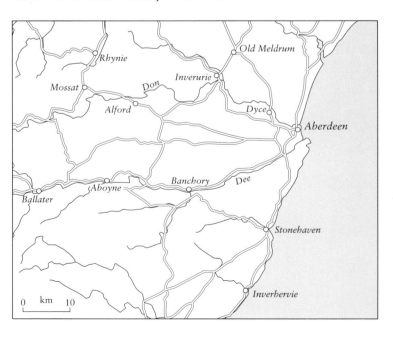

have been at Aberdour Bay, where there is a St Drostan's Well and a ruined medieval church of St Drostan on the road down to the bay. The early church at Rathen was dedicated to St Ethernan, and the den on the east side of Mormend Hill is called St Ethernan's Slack.

The later monks of Deer, influenced by the prestige of the Columban Church since the time of Kenneth MacAlpin, claimed St Columba as their original founder. There is also a confusion between Columba and Colm, as at the seaside village of St Combs, where the ruined chapel by the shore is now called St Columba's rather than St Colm's.

Banffshire Settlements

The inland site of Old Deer indicates that though many of the Early Saints arrived in Banff and Buchan by sea, they settled fertile riverside sites where agriculture provided their main support.

Travelling west from Deer, you cross the old county boundary at Turriff. The first church at Turriff was dedicated to St Comgan, while south of Turriff at Kirktown of Auchterless the ancient dedication was to St Donnan. These western Saints sailed round the north of Scotland or by currach up the Great Glen.

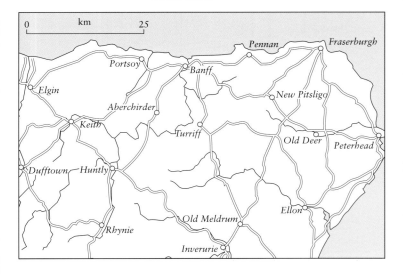

A little further down the River Deveron, a mile west of Turriff, is the peaceful site of St Eunan's Chapel in a graveyard above the river. 'Eunan' is a version of St Adomnan and this was an important Columban foundation. The Brecbennach of St Columba, later known as the Monymusk Reliquary, was kept here indicating that this was the principal site of the Columban mission. Adomnan's route north was through Badenoch and Strathspey.

South-west of Aberchirder is the Kirkton of Marnoch, where the old church of St Marnoch was at the graveyard beside the river. St Marnoc was the Saint of Kilmarnock and of St Marnoc's Island off Bute from where he voyaged north in the tradition of the Early Saints seeking a new frontier. He is believed to be buried at Marnoch. The present church, on a rise to the north, was built inside a stone circle indicating the pre-Christian significance of this site.

Continuing west, the first church at Keith was founded by St Maelrubha of Applecross, adding yet another independent strand to the northern Pictish missions. The original church site is in Old Keith on the eastern bank of the River Isla, but only a mound and some masonry fragments remain of a later medieval church of Maelrubha.

Turning north-west to Dufftown, Mortlach Church half a mile south of the town was established by St Moluag of Lismore. Although the fabric here is medieval with modern reconstruction, there is clear evidence of occupation since Pictish times.

Lossiemouth and Kinneddar

Elgin Cathedral was the 'Lantern of the North' and its splendid ruins explain why, but Moray's earliest Christian roots lie elsewhere. North of Elgin, past the older medieval cathedral site of Spynie, is Kinneddar Churchyard just south of the main entrance to RAF. Lossiemouth. A number of early Pictish stones were found here including sections of a shrine, which can be seen in Elgin Museum. The quality of this shrine suggests an important early monastery.

The Saint whose relics were revered at Kinneddar was probably St Gerardine, an Irish missionary. His tiny cave was above the esplanade in Lossiemouth but long since destroyed. Here he used to keep a light to guide the fishermen in over the sandbanks, and their gratitude is recorded in several coastal names including Halliman (Holy Man) Skerries and Halliman Head where Gerardine had another cave retreat.

Burghead

West of Lossiemouth was the massive Pictish fort and harbour of Burghead. Many of the huge ramparts have been overlaid by the modern town but the inner fortress or upper ward survives on the headland. The striking Burghead Bulls were carved here and may have had ritual significance as part of a Pictish fertility cult.

Equally impressive is the Burghead Well, a large pool in a rock-cut chamber reached by a flight of steps through a low crag. Originally providing the fort's water supply, this pool may have been used as a baptistery in Christian times. Fragments of an early Christian shrine were found in the old cemetery near the top of Grant Street, and they can be viewed in Burghead Library along with two of the bulls.

Sueno's Stone and Rodney's Stone

North of Forres near Findhorn Bay is a *tour de force* of Pictish carving, Sueno's Stone. On one side there is a ring-headed cross with interlaced spiral knotwork. On the other is a bloody catalogue of conflict and carnage. An unknown battle is recorded here in vivid detail.

Further west at Brodie Castle is another important Pictish stone with a cross and the familiar Pictish symbols. There are also three inscriptions in the early ogam alphabet on the stone, including the name Ethernan. The stone came originally from the old churchyard at nearby Dyke, which may have been another missionary settlement of St Ethernan.

Birnie

Travelling back towards Elgin, a minor road from Crook of Alves wanders southeast to Birnie. A short detour from this road leads to the restored medieval Abbey of Pluscarden, where a Benedictine community maintains the spirit and ethos of the Early Saints.

The old church at Birnie is dedicated to St Brendan the Voyager and may represent an original foundation. An Early Saint's handbell - the Ronnel Bell - is kept at the manse and there are a number of Pictish carvings in the churchyard wall. In the River Spey, over the hill near Knockando House is a pool named Pulvrennan or St Brendan's Pool, which may have been used for baptisms in the open-air style of the first missionaries.

Strathspey

Part of Moray's strategic importance lies in its position at the end of Strathspey, a vital route across Badenoch to Loch Laggan, Glen Spean and the Great Glen. Travelling south-west, upriver past Knockando, there are suggestions of early Christian sites in the farm names of Auchnahannet north of the river and at Achnahannet north-west of Dulnain Bridge, but no visible remains.

In Badenoch itself, the first church at Kincraig one mile south of the village, was dedicated to St Drostan, while in the currently used Insh Church east of Kincraig there is an early Saint's handbell which is associated with St Adomnan, to whom the church is dedicated. Here the Saints of east and west meet on their travels.

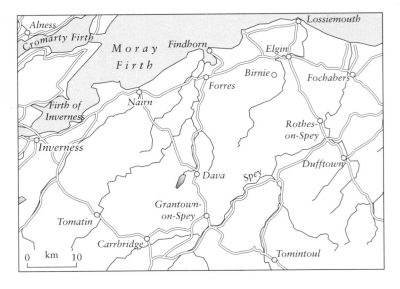

The old ruined church at Kingussie is in a small glen west of the town and was dedicated to St Columba. A later carved panel reads in Gaelic 'My Druid is Christ the Son of God'.

The Great Glen and Loch Laggan

Soon after his arrival in Scotland St Columba, with St Kenneth and St Comgall, travelled up the Great Glen to the capital of Brude, King of the Northern Picts, seeking his support for their new monasteries. Much of the journey would be by currach. Beyond Fort William an alternative route north is offered by Glen Spean and Loch Laggan. At the head of the loch on the north side is the old burial ground of St Cainnech or Kenneth. Four miles further east, where the Spey joins the River Moshie, the Pictish fortress of Dun-na-Lamh rises 600 feet above the valley.

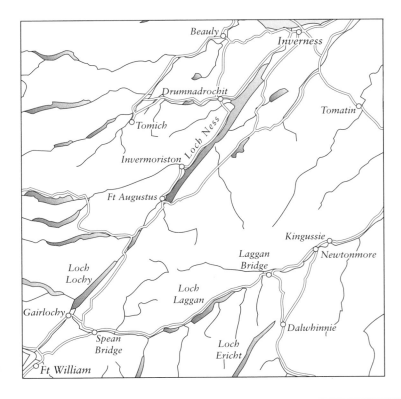

At the southern end of Loch Ness in the Great Glen is Fort Augustus, a name imposed by the Hanoverian rulers on Kilcumein or the Church of Cumin, who was successor to Columba as Abbot of Iona. The site of the military barracks here is now a Benedictine Abbey, which also houses an excellent visitor centre telling the story of Fort Augustus and of the early Celtic monasteries. In the course of his journey up Loch Ness, Columba encountered a sea monster which he conquered with the sign of the Cross.

On the northern shore of Loch Ness, Urquhart Castle guards the approach to Glen Urquhart. Within the castle walls are the remains of a Pictish fort where Columba baptised a chieftain and his son. The early church sites here include Kilmore, east of Drumnadrochit, which was originally connected with St Drostan, and the former Kil St Ninian above Temple Pier, which owes its name to a medieval foundation of the Knights Templar. A clearly attested Saint in this area is a little known St Finian, to whom the old church at

Abriachan on the north side of Loch Ness and Dunlichit in Strathnairn to the south were dedicated.

At Inverness itself, Columba met King Brude and confronted Broichan the Druid. Whether the site of these encounters was at Craig Phadrig, the fortress overlooking the Beauly Firth, is unclear but this dramatic location seems appropriate.

Rosemarkie and Fortrose

At Rosemarkie the parish church is on the site of a Celtic monastery founded first by St Moluag and later developed by St Curitan. A fine Pictish cross-slab, the Rosemarkie Stone, was found here and can be viewed in the Groam House Museum. There is a tradition that St Curitan, also known as Boniface, was buried at Rosemarkie.

The religious importance of this site was recognised by the foundation of the medieval Abbey of Fortrose around which the town of Fortrose still clusters.

Tain

Coming at the end of the missionary age, St Duthac has left a clear impression on his home town. The early chapel of St Duthac, to the east of the town at the modern cemetery, is traditionally supposed to mark the place of his birth and probably indicates the later site of his burial and shrine. The sacred shirt of Duthac, believed to give protection in battle, was also kept here. St Duthac's Collegiate Church in the town later housed the Saint's relics and became an important centre of pilgrimage, supported among others by James IV.

Portmahomack

The peninsula east of Tain was an important Pictish and Christian centre well before the time of Duthac. Many early carved stones have been found here including the elaborate carved cross at Nigg Parish Church and the outstanding Hilton of Cadboll Stone, which is now in the Royal Museum of Scotland in Edinburgh. The name Portmahomack means 'Port of Colman or Colmac' and currently a major excavation is uncovering a Pictish settlement around Tarbat Old Parish Church above the village. The church itself is believed to be built above an earlier chapel, and among the cross-slabs found in the graveyard is one with an inscription to Rethaide, Abbot of Fearn. This may refer to a Celtic monastery which was sited somewhere west of Edderton. Fearn Abbey at Hill of Fearn is a medieval ruin. Archaeology is unlocking another chapter of Scotland's early Christian story at Portmahomack.

Dornoch

The first church at Dornoch was founded by St Finbarr of Barra and Cork, but the early Celtic origins of the site are now overlaid by the solid medieval Cathedral of Dornoch.

Urquhart Castle

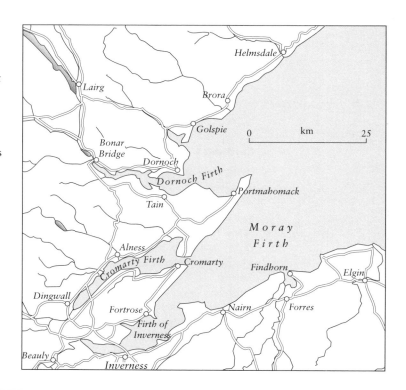

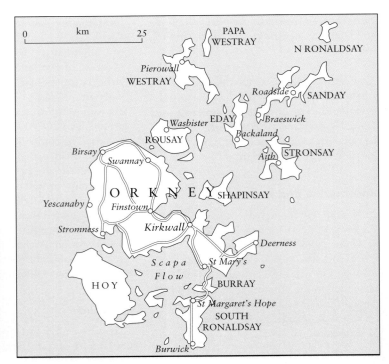

Brough of Birsay

From Dornoch inland routes lead up into the mountains, straths and lochs of Sutherland. At Creich on the north side of the Dornoch Firth, east of the Pictish fort at Dun Creich, the church was dedicated to St Devenick, and 'St Devhan's Cross' still stands here. On the south side of the Firth was the Celtic monastery of Fearn, but its exact site is unknown.

Caithness

In the time of the Early Saints the Pictish kingdom of Cait embraced most of what we now know as Sutherland as well as Caithness. The whole area was subject to Norse settlement, which has obscured its early missionary roots.

The Saints of Buchan - Drostan, Fergus, Medan and Colm - were all active in Caithness. Near Durness, east of Cape Wrath at Balnakeil Bay, Durness Old Church is an early site. Further east, the old Church of Farr at Bettyhill has a Pictish cross-slab and, to the north-west of Farr Bay, Eilean Coomb is named after St Colm.

The Thurso Museum has some early Pictish crosses including one from Halkirk, south of Thurso, where the old parish church has associations with both St Fergus and St Drostan. There is a fine interlaced cross west of Thurso at Reay, where the church was dedicated to St Colm. St Fergus is associated with Wick and St Medan with Freswick on the north-eastern coast of Caithness, while west of John O'Groats, Canisbay Church is another early church site dedicated to Drostan.

There is a tradition that St Maelrubha of Applecross was killed by the Norsemen at Skail in Strath Naver and this must have been the fate of many early missionaries. However Christianity soon took root among the settlers. The first notable convert was Queen Aud 'the deep-minded'. According to a later saga,

' *Aud was in Caithness when she heard tell of (her son) Thorstein's death. She had a ship built secretly in the forest, and once she was ready hoisted sail for Orkney'.*

Later Aud set off for Iceland where

'She made her home at Hvamm and had a place for her devotions at Krossholar, for she had been baptized and held strongly to the Christian faith.'

Orkney

In his Life of Columba, Adomnan tells us about one of the first voyaging Saints to reach the Northern Isles.

'On another occasion, Cormac, the soldier of Christ .... was seeking for a second time, to find a hermitage in the ocean; leaving land he had pressed on for many days, at full sail, across the boundless sea. St Columba, who was staying beyond Druimalban, commended him to Brude, the King, in the presence of the sub-King of the Orkneys .... The Saint spoke in this manner because he knew in spirit that the same Cormac would come, after many months, to Orkney.'

Perhaps tradition is correct in saying that the earliest Christian settlement was on Papa Westray to the north, where there was a monastery at Munkerhouse. But little is visible here apart from the later settlement at St Tredwell's Loch, which has a medieval dedication to Triduana. A better impression of the first missionaries is gained at the Brough of Deerness on the Mainland east of Kirkwall. Here the layout of the monastery with its rectangular cells is quite clear, though access to the Brough is now difficult due to the collapse of the land bridge.

The Brough of Birsay, twenty miles north-west of Kirkwall, was an important Christian centre in Pictish and Viking times. Access is by a tidal causeway. The site includes an early monastery and the later St Peter's Cathedral built by Thorfinn the Mighty, the Norse Earl of Orkney. St Magnus was buried here before his relics were transferred to Kirkwall.

Birsay is a transitional site which heralds the Norse Christian culture which flourished on Orkney and Shetland. This is evident at several places including Eynhallow (Holy Island) near Rousay (car ferry from Tingwall) and the Round Church at Orphir near Kirkwall. Its most poignant memorial however is St Magnus Church on Egilsay (car ferry from Tingwall), where Thorfinn's grandson Magnus was treacherously murdered by his brother Haakon. A monument marks the spot, just south of the church with its Hiberno-Norse round tower.

It was in honour of Magnus, the martyr of peace, that St Magnus Cathedral in Kirkwall was built. There the Saint's remains, including his pierced skull, still rest within one of the Cathedral's massive piers. No Scottish cathedral retains so complete a sense of its original integrity and purpose.

Shetland

The principal monastic site on the Shetland Islands may have been at Papil on West Burra, south-west of Lerwick. The Monks Stone from Papil, which is on view at the Shetland Museum in Lerwick, shows a procession of five monks moving towards a High Cross. Four are on foot and one (the Abbot?) on a pony but each carries a crozier and a book satchel for their Gospel manuscript.   These are the Early Saints of Shetland, but we do not know their names. The stone is the side panel of a shrine which was reverenced at Papil. The Papil Stone, another Pictish sculpture from this site, also depicts these monks below a wheel-headed cross with a variety of Pictish symbols.

The carved corner posts of a similar shrine were uncovered at St Ninian's Isle, which is reached by an isthmus from the Mainland south of West Burra. A Pictish treasure hoard of ornate silver was also discovered at this early monastic site, probably buried by the monks under the altar of their

Eynhallow Church

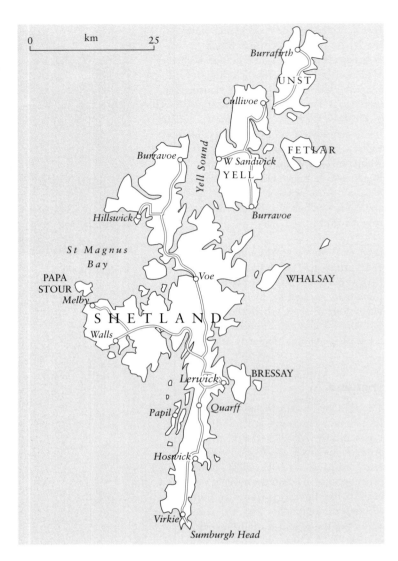

church during the Viking raids. Replicas are on show in the Shetland Museum; the originals are in the Royal Museum of Scotland in Edinburgh.

The Early Saints also sought 'places of resurrection' in the remoter islands such as Papa Stour which means 'the Great Island of the Priests'. Erosion and the powerful action of the sea are constantly changing these coasts, but substantial early monasteries have been surveyed at Birrier on Yell, where the land bridge is all but worn away (fourteen buildings); and at Outer Brough, a rock stack off Fetlar where sixteen building foundations can be traced along with a stone wall defining the cashel on the landward side. In the far north, at the Kame of Isbister on Unst, nineteen building foundations survive but others have been lost to the ocean.

These remote sanctuaries of the waves have left no written or carved communication and are virtually inaccessible except by helicopter. Yet they are still eloquent of their original spiritual purpose.

NORTH WESTERN FRONTIERS

Ardnamurchan

From the perspective of the Early Saints the peninsula of Ardnamurchan could have been an island, since its importance was as a landfall on the sea routes north. The church at Kilchoan on the sheltered south-west coast was dedicated to St Comgan. East of the ruined church of Kilchoan is St Columba's burial ground and well at Camus nan Geall. Adomnan's biography tells of Columba baptising an infant here and also of how Columba defended one of his flock by driving a persecuting raider into the sea at 'the sharp bay of Ardnamurchan'.

Eigg, Rum and Canna

These three islands, all reached from Mallaig, provide stepping stones on the Saints' routes north.

Eigg is remarkable as the scene of the earliest recorded martyrdom of a Celtic Saint, when St Donnan and his whole community of monks were massacred here on Easter Sunday 16th April 618, apparently by a local Pictish queen who resented their settlement. The ruined chapel of Donnan is at the end of a deep gap which divides the island from Laig to Kildonnan.

Rum is traditionally associated with the hermit Saint Bec or Beccan but little trace of his occupation remains on this wild, mountainous island, which was cleared of its entire population in 1826 and only partially resettled.

Canna by contrast is a gentle fertile island. Canna's associations are with Columba and

Iona rather than the quite separate mission of Donnan to the northern Picts. The ruined chapel of St Columba is at A'Chill and there is also an early carved cross shaft in the modern church. On the southern coast below Am Beannan there is a monastic ruin on the foreshore, isolated by rocks and sea. The name Sgor nam Ban-Naomha or Skerry of the Holy Woman suggests a woman's 'dysart' or retreat. The modern Catholic chapel is on the tidal island of Sanday.

Skye (East)

Skye presents over nine hundred miles of coastline and is the geographical key to the north-west. It is for this reason that the surviving Celtic sites are distributed along the two sea channels to the west and east while Isle Ornsay - the island of St Oran - in the Sound of Sleat watches over the southern approaches with its lighthouse and ruined chapel.

On the eastern side of Skye off Broadford Bay is Pabay or Priest's Isle which has an

early ruined chapel of uncertain date. Next, off Loch Ainort, is the island of Scalpay which also has a ruined chapel beside Scalpay House. The most interesting of these islands however is the next northwards, Raasay, which is reached by car ferry from Sconser on Skye.

Near Raasay House the ruined Celtic Chapel is dedicated to St Moluag of Lismore, whose progress can be traced from here to Kilmaluag ('the church of Moluag') at the northern tip of Skye. On the shore beside the chapel is a Celtic cross carved in the rock, while beside the House is a Pictish symbol stone carved with a cross of Maltese form and the vestiges of the chi/ro symbol of Christ.

North of Raasay is the island of Rona, sometimes called South Rona to distinguish it from Rona north of Lewis. This Rona has a ruined chapel, An Teampuill, built with rubble and shell lime. On the east of the island the Giant's Cave seems also to have been used as an early place of worship. Rona is now uninhabited.

Further north on Skye itself is the main town, Portree, which owes its prominence to its fine natural harbour. On a tidal island off Portree is the ruined chapel of St Columba.

Skye (West)

Circling the Trotternish peninsula at the north end of Skye past Kilmaluig and Duntulm Castle, the road turns south to Kilmuir where the old church and graveyard, and the Skye Museum of Island Life, provide the main focus of interest. South of Kilmuir however, on the right-hand side of the road, lies the drained Loch Chaluim Chille or St Columba's Loch. A stony mound now marks the former island of Columba. The foundations of the enclosing wall, beehive cells and two chapels can still be seen on the mound.

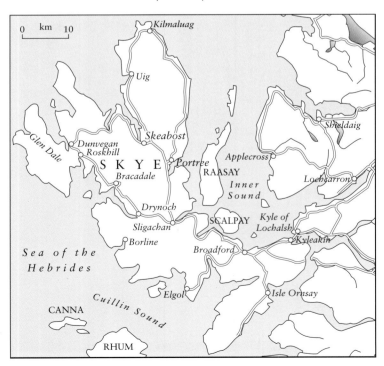

Further south, near the head of Loch Snizort Beag, is the little village of Skeabost tucked in beside the hotel. In the mouth of the river is St Columba's Island with the ruins of a Celtic and a medieval chapel. Believed to be an original Columban foundation, the island was the headquarters of the Bishopric of the Isles from 1079 to 1498, and the burial place of the Nicolsons.

On Skye's second northern peninsula, Vaternish, a mile north of Fairy Bridge, is Annait or 'Mother Church' which is one of the oldest Christian settlements on the island. The monastery was built on a promontory between two deep gulleys through which the burns cascade. The cashel wall is quite clear, with the foundations of a chapel and several beehive cells. The site has not been excavated and its founding saint remains unknown.

Skye's third northern peninsula, Duirinish, spreads westwards from Dunvegan with its magnificent castle and sheltered loch. In Duirinish the valley of Glendale gathers together several crofting townships as it opens out to the Minch and the outer isles, making it a useful landfall in the long seaway from Ireland to the far north. Glendale was a centre of the Druidic religion and Columba came here to establish Christianity. An early graveyard stands at the foot of the valley and on the level ground beside the river are the displaced boundary stones of a lost monastery. The earliest known dedication here is to St Comgan.

In the south-west of Skye at Borline on Loch Eynort is another important site of early Christian settlement. Kilmoruy was St Maelrubha's church, related to the famous monastery at Applecross. The shaft of a Celtic High Cross still stands in the graveyard depicting the crucifixion on one side and an abbot on the other. This is probably a later portrayal of Maelrubha, one of the greatest missionary saints to establish a base on Skye.

Lochalsh to Applecross

On the mainland in the district of Lochalsh, the early church sites of Kilchoan and Kilillan commemorate St Comgan and St Fillan respectively. Comgan's sister St Kentigerna, mother of Fillan, also worked in the area as part of this remarkable family of Saints who were related to the royal house of Leinster in Ireland.

The road north from Lochalsh was not a conduit for the early Saints whose preferred route was by sea, putting in at the lochs which indent the north-western coast. On the coast looking across to Raasay was Maelrubha's principal monastery at Applecross, which was linked not with Iona but with Bangor in Ireland. Travelling cross-country to Applecross over the spectacular pass of Bealach nam Bo (pass of the cattle), you realise that in practical terms the coastal plain was an island.

At one time the monastery's sanctuary area extended for six miles, and the village is still known in Gaelic as A'Chomraich or Sanctuary. North of the village the road rounds the bay to Applecross Chapel. The burial ground here is the only visible remnant of this once strategic monastery, and may be the Saint's last resting place. Applecross was destroyed by the Vikings within a century of Maelrubha's death.

Loch Maree

North of Loch Torridon is the loch which is believed to derive its name from Maelrubha. Isle of Maree, which lies close to the north side of the loch, has the foundations of an early chapel and a filled-in well. This was probably Maelrubha's retreat and may have been a pre-Christian religious site. Isle Maree is also claimed as the Saint's burial place. It can only be visited by arrangement with the warden of the Beinn Eighe National Nature Reserve through the visitor centre at Anancaun near Kinlochewe.

From Loch Maree, Maelrubha's influence extended north round the coast of Sutherland, though then as now the population seems to have been relatively sparse, and no traces of an important early Christian site have been uncovered in this mountain fastness.

Barra

To the west of Skye the sea road of the Saints begins with Barra and its scattering of islands. The southernmost landfall on the chain of the Outer Hebrides is Berneray, which is now dominated by the Barra Head Lighthouse. On MacLean's Point there is the site of an early chapel and burial ground. Pabbay too has traces of an early chapel at the White Bay or Bagh Ban.

On Barra itself, the ancient religious centre is in the north of the island at Cille-Bharra or Kilbarr - the church of Barr or Findbarr, Patron Saint of Cork. Beautifully sited on the green hillside of Ben Eoligarry, Kilbarr looks out over the Sound to Fuday, and

Eriskay and South Uist beyond. The cashel wall survives along with the ruined church and two chapels, all of an early period. With its distinctive Irish and Norse connections, Kilbarr represents another independent strand in Scotland's early missionary story.

Kilbarr remained a popular place of pilgrimage into the medieval period, while reverence for the local saint has never been lost on Barra. In the words of a very old Irish poem,

Barr, the fire of wisdom, loves
Humility to the men of the world;
He never saw in want
A person that he did not assist.

The Uists

North and South Uist, with Benbecula between, were power centres of the medieval Lordship of the Isles and then of Clan Donald. Consequently the early missionary sites have been largely overlaid by medieval churches which are themselves in a sad state of ruin.

On South Uist the principal site is at Howmore near the west coast. There were originally five churches or chapels here, but only St Columba's Church has significant visible remains. On Benbecula is another St Columba's Church or Teampull Chaluim Cille, near Balivanich. In addition to the substantial ruins there is a St Columba's Well, and nearby a small cairn made of stones which were brought to the well as votive offerings.

Perhaps the most interesting of this sequence of ruins is Teampull na Triconaid on the Carinish peninsula at the south-western corner of North Uist. Trinity Church was built by Bethog, the medieval Prioress of Iona. There is also a detached side chapel which is reached by a vaulted passage from the main church.

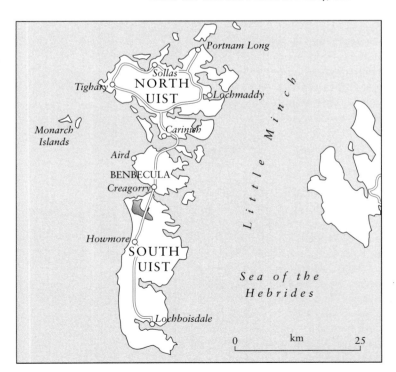

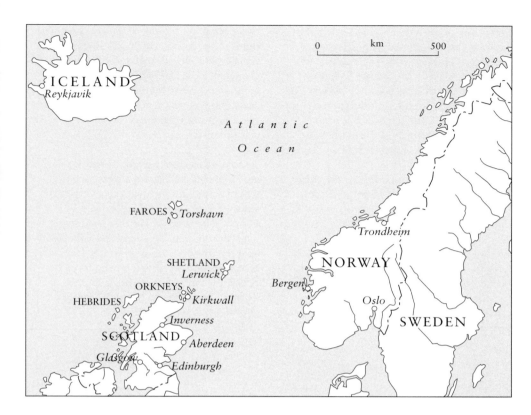

Five miles off Hougharry Point in North Uist are the low-lying Monach Islands. Ceann Ear was the site of an early nunnery, while the monks of Shillay were responsible for keeping a light to guide sailors. All of the islands are now uninhabited.

The Long Island

Together Harris and Lewis constitute the largest island in Britain and the furthest north-western fringe of the British Isles. This was also a spiritual and geographical frontier for the early Saints seeking 'the ends of the earth'. From here they sailed to Caithness, Orkney, Shetland, the Faroes, Iceland and Greenland. Then, in a reverse movement, Norse settlers came to Lewis and Harris, some to stay and some to migrate further to Iceland.

Because of later Norse influence the Celtic missionary sites are often no more than a heap of grass-covered stones remembered only by name. Such places include Teampull Eoin at Bragar, Teampull Pheadair at Shader, Teampull Bhrigid at Mid-Borve, Teampull nan Cro Naomh at Galson and the island of Colum Cille in Loch Erisort, as well as early settlements on the Shiant Islands, and the Flannans, where a tiny drystone cell called Teampull Beannachadh stands by the lighthouse. St Kilda was also a monk's landfall, though its name derives from the Norse *skildir* or 'distant place' and not from a saint. By contrast, the later medieval church of St Clement at Rodel in the south of Harris and the much earlier Callanish Stones on Lewis have survived to give a much better idea of their importance as religious centres. On the Eye peninsula east of Stornoway the Ui Chapel is dedicated to St Columba.

To capture the atmosphere of the early Celtic missionaries, travel north to Ness on the Butt of Lewis. At Eorpaidh Tempull Mholuaidh is a Norse Christian foundation on the site of a Celtic mission settlement dedicated to or founded by St Moluag of Lismore. The Norse Christian culture of Lewis is brilliantly evoked by the Lewis Chessmen which were found in 1831 in Uig Sands, and are displayed in the summer months in the Museum Nan Eilean in Stornoway. The church at Eorpaidh was dedicated in Norse times to St Olaf.

In Moluag's time, Eorpaidh was the cultic centre of a sea god called Shony whose festival was observed here, centuries after the arrival of Christianity, on 1st November, when a cup of ale was symbolically cast into the water to ensure fertility. The Saint himself was believed to heal both limbs and lunatics.

Little remains of another chapel at Eorpaidh, Teampull Ronain, but its

existence points to the island of Rona forty miles to the north. On North Rona a remakable Celtic chapel and cell survive the elements. Even at Eorpaidh Ronan's companions were mainly the birds and the seals, but he pushed north seeking 'a desert place in the sea' and was carried to Rona by a sea monster.

According to local legend, Ronan was accompanied by his two sisters, one of whom travelled south-west to the rocky stack of Sula Sgeir where she lived as a hermit. The ruins of another hermitage, Tigh Beann çche, do survive on Sula Sgeir, scoured by wind, spray and rain. Here is a forcible reminder of Saints who loved 'a prison of hard stone, to bring all into heaven'. Boat trips to North Rona are entirely weather dependent.